The Bridge

ric
hool

THE COLLECTIVE PRESS

Cover design
& Layout

Cataloguing In Publication Data for this book is available
from the British Library

ISBN 1 899449 70 1

Published with the financial support of the
Arts Council of Wales.

Cover photograph by John Jones

Main Typeface; Arial 10pt.

Printed in Great Britain by Redwood Books

The Bridge

To

Peg, Bill, Mike, Sue & Peter

Never let me come home a stranger.

contents

Something as Beautiful as This!

Window mouths hung open with curtain tongues
shout across Newport railway yard
drawn into light and a whistle starts!
Walking, hands in pockets, blinking,

day comes to order as a newspaper kiosk
preening itself in layers, one on one with headlines
jutted for taking to a train, to a job
or else to mop minutes of waiting.

Sounds skid across the street,
a stylus slid across a record. Hear them
in helloes and things understood
in a shorthand, affirmed: "And You!".

A cigarette ground hard
into the pavement of a new day.

Saturday.

Going to the bookstall
know it is Saturday
after Friday night with friends
                              trading
sparks of conversation
                    a suitcase of experience
            a kiss
to twinkle darkness
                        like wonder
I am my own child playing
                imagination's detritus
speaking first important words
                            & hearing
a language   inanimate things
                the sentiment of rocks
                                replacing taint
        a paint-flaked wall

Going to the bookstall
know it is Saturday
                unlocking night
                        each different key
enjoying   music of argument
                    conflict's symphony
                            wind & tree
                        rain & roof
                unsheltered
I have Tarzan's belief
                his primitive call
                        BEAUTIFUL
Saturday at the bookstall

Private Life in a Tumble-Drier.

A single
    tumbled
        item
           churns
knotting & twisting itself

Up & dropped
up & dropped
in each revolution
variations of sound

The time device works
                absolutely
the world halted
in a slump & last button scrape

Almost square & white
its mouth
its iris
one pouted stare

Seven years I am here
in a holiday home
on the south side of Blaina

If the telephone could talk
it would say
NOT AT HOME

urgent unanswered
beside a bonsai myrtle
tiptoed on roots
silently growing

Seven years I am here
in a holiday home
on the south side of Blaina

The window view is buddleia filled
warm with mallow
                              & I'm reading William Burroughs
                                   more
chilling than January

Snow is a partner
quiet in mornings
                    suppressing all sounds

Summer murmurs
all noise is background

Le Thérapeute sits
                with his stick
sheltered from night his daylight
cloaked and hatted
an eye at a window
day upon night
                each
shadows itself

Here my spin-drier
                seven years
in a holiday home
on the south side of Blaina

Deserts in Spain I have driven
in night-time
                too many
nights I have spent in deserts
                            how many
ants inhabit the earth

I am a visitor
                            though this is a whisper
Is South Wales a park
                & ride zone
along M4 to London

Never ignored
                Japanese
have car plants

Some kid has paint-sprayed
the R out of Rhondda
& SOME KID has paint sprayed
I luv u dweebie
on the side of a bridge

I believe I have LIVED
                now EXIST

like washing stirring
tumble-dried in my holiday home
Blaina

Le Thérapeute by René Magritte.

Night Hawk.

Desertion leaves me on the night street.
Houses crumple like pack ice,
windows sliced shut.

A face inside the glass
is a portrait of loneliness -
darkness its mirror.

And good souls sleep. Vulnerable
doors studded with bells
can stop a resting heart.

A dustbin lid, rattled off by an urban fox,
swallows its sound to still.
A roundabout hung over with orange light,

plays solitaire. Slight objections
soundtracked, slow
with slap-back echo,

register off a mansard roof
and guttering
excited by hits of rain.

Urban Walking Through my Head.

Roads stroll off
stalk past houses
                    pushed
behind squared gardens geometric with flowers

Pass on & pass
ever open gates
a leftover fence
                    leans
roots buckle paving
A Cossack attack against urbanization

Amble Avenue

An air show makes its aircraft noise
knocks heads back
pencilling eyes into oriental lines of search

With two barrels of fingers & one cocked thumb
a kid instinctively attempts to shoot the bomber down
It veers taking his flak back to enthusiasts

Houses shuffled shoulder to shoulder
anticipate a scrum

A car is parked
hi
       &
             lo
kerb
       &
             road
its bonnet warm
enough to stretch a naked back

A window slid open like an easy trombone
trickles music
             as heat
                 takes off my jacket
pegs it on a finger over my shoulder

                           Woman
smokes
on the doorstep of an open purple door
digs a furrow of skirt
between legs
             watches my documentary stare

                        Young boy
lopes
palming a basket ball down
Its sound slaps off walls

assembles a figure
in the nephritic eye of a bay window

Swollen sunglasses are planets on the face
silks whisper around the body
Quickly it evaporates

Three shops of silence advertise
blanched windows of closure

A large cardboard colour figure fades
blues
       to
           greens
yellows
       to
           creams

Only spiders work

Bricks moulder from pointing

A scallop roof tile prised open
has a green lip of moss

Over-sunned paint exfoliates

Dockyards lick the air
the slack river not far   somewhere
a train shakes its way

This road
beyond the range of the cowboy builder
       nods to sleep
I predict its wakening complete as a fairy tale
in the kiss of the demolition crane

All is hot
    slow
    forgotten

s a t o u t like a l o n g a f t e r n o o n

Millennium Statement for a South Wales' Valley Town.

This the place gone
Forgotten
      A dream
           Uncounted
the flung down pavements of accident
rupture and jut and trip
        or
sink in thirsty water

Houses slur valley sides
pressed beneath a stuttered threat
rockfalls gather like bad weather

Here forgotten wealth Victorian
in an Institute of red brick and lavatera split sandstone
Its slate roof begged with grass-tuft-gutters

Here the road once-a-week swept
crushed cans and angry glass are medals

Here the spectre of a shop window
eyeballs a disused High Street
           HERE
sat on a wall of addiction
spiked in an arm
        broken
children play in the sandpit of the new millennium

From Four Till Late.

I hear frost fingering its filigree
across the pond of another affair;
Know the thickening of resentment
prevents attempts to cut fishing holes.

It is a deceptively white landscape
yearning for movement - a scurry,
hop, a rolling of warmth,
a thaw of spring attitudes.

But ice chinks in lonely drinks at this bar.
Love's potion grips blue flesh,
the beat suggests a dredging action
in sync with the voice of Robert Johnson.

Robert Johnson: seminal blues singer.
'From Four Till Late': a song by Johnson.

Pilgrimage.

Another road cut up and I'm moving like a blade
parried past the tick of cones and red and white sticks
clicked into the cat's-eye pads.

Time warps against the skin of the car.
Northwards Celsius diminishes
as my heart warms. The mile-cracked dance tightens hands

on the throat of the wheel. The landscape moves
between dismal & grim - no fairy tale.
A heap of promises buried under spoil,

winding gear and BIG TALK on a face
in the Affiliated Club. I breathe
a mephitic breeze: river; engineering; oil.

My compulsive tongue reshapes phrase & lilt;
a gravitational pull realigns
concerns dispersed by geography & time.

The Bridge.

It's a misconception;
the bridge keeps places apart,
there is little connection.

Always blown
like fetters released
in war zones

or used to transfuse
arterial needs until dry
and no use.

It quivers like a gymnast
on rings, crucified, hating
the pain at arms-length.

Imagine, born
on the western carriage of the Severn span
in no-mans-land,

no country of origin,
suspended for a lifetime
by roadworks.

Plea to a Wanton Muse on a World Holiday with only an Overnight Suitcase and a Penchant for Six Changes a Day.

I can't hear you - haven't for a while
like I used to. For example today
striding away and really giving the breeze what for
as the evening-bled sun juiced the ramshackle grasses
which parted every so often as a gust sliced by
exposing the odd grouse, face stupid with alarm,
an "O" rebounded from eye to eye
and its tongue swallowed in fright.

I can't hear you, like I did,
rattle over the boards in a squall;
planish the lake in a swelter of beats,
retreat, return from another direction
to flatten the unready sheet,
throw the tensed rope slack around its pin and me
left heeled into the wind all untrimmed.

I don't hear you demon in my sleeping ear
churning sleep into cheese, or running
autistic from wall to wall, or crawl
clawing your way back into the womb,
nor eavesdrop the suck of your dejected thumb - no
retort from your vindictive tongue.

Can't hear you explode like a Colt exercised
by its hairline trigger - I don't want that fixed.
Want all chambers loaded and easy
on the hip ready for a leather-slapped show down
or have me hit, dry-gulched for desertion
on other business. The sun
always at zenith: *Do not forsake me*
oh my darling...

My Heart, Modern Art and Drinking.

The octopus in my chest
still has a hunger, thank god;
white-hot corpuscles abrading its blue skin,
burning the sticky horrors left
by cupidity's last outing.

Love comes like a cubist painting,
all dimensions exposed at once:
a maze of angles, attitudes,
without a natural focus.
It hits me to the floor.

Love's rush, then urgent doubts,
the woman's flatfish face, her eye
off countenance, become nightmare.
Whisky-shaped order regulates
the offbeat heart; love to perspective.

Ophthalmic Appointment.

He looked into my eyes without looking
for my soul. Flashing lights -
as if from a passage by A.C. Clarke.
Such brilliance holds no meaning,
only awe, only
light,
silverwhitebright and empty.

Even peeling back my onion-skin lids, I forgave him:
his job, blunt fingers working
surfaces too delicate for a whisper's imprint
bullied into submission, denied
the briefest blink.
The room's dry atmosphere a double agent.

"Granulations." He washed the word
over my face, panning for a find
and another scintillant nail stole
secrets. He already knew
parts taken for granted.
                I marvelled propositions:
the vascular hills and nerve-cleft cliffs,
cut in suspicion. The regular air
breathed from his nostrils, past my lips - sure,
so close, he could kiss my gently tilted face.

Bottle

Run - we must -
the rain makes our steps
a dance of dryness.

Let us hold hands,
be
an apology away from crushed fingers.

Reality a Constable painting?
... We'd not be in it.

Our vistas the shaken dusters of pampas grass
in a button-pinched Welsh November,
pelted pavements and the corner shop
where I am a shadow choosing the bottle
in which I will empty myself,

where you are a wasp
bumping against a pane of glass.

A Garden Sequence.

1. *patio furniture*

The last, last-year's coffee ring
still on the table.

Collapsible laughter
clicked upright.

I shall sit through this summer,
darken as the furniture fades;

steal mornings
in this walled cell of sunlight.

2. *family business*

The sun, pinched
through the parasol hole,

explodes upon the dark planet
cast by the plastic's roundness.

Radiant lines imprint the tabletop:
a pie chart allocating seating.

Velcro lips rip instructions
about the evening do.

I ask Aunt Who?
And a nephew I shall never remember.

Family business,
extruded and brittle as uncooked spaghetti.

Plastic is so soulless,
so necessary.

3. *air*

So much sky - none of it silent.
A 'plane frays a seam of denim.

A starling restarts
a passing sound.

There Icarus controls his Dacron sheet,
it cracks on air, riding

land's riposte
to the sun's heat.

A panic of wasp
thrashes.

4. *weather*

On the radio: *The driest spring*.
The turn of the standpipe creaks

from East Sussex; the scrape of a bucket
nudged by the wind.

A Dedication to Alan Hull.

Northern music skirls
corridors of social injustice.

Artistic madness ticks
in the time-bomb of Pop

A melody led you
and lyrics marched

to the opposite end of a smile,
to the pit of an empty stomach.

TO YOU a glass raised in song:
sour and sweet tears.

This whereabouts not Tyneside
but memory riveted to a place-name

as casual as bus destination
or Metro stop.

Of Sound and Person.

I come from a place where sea is ALWAYS
in your ears. In all weathers hear
its hours open and close
the horseshoe bay of rock and sand
or slop over oily-haired weed
in the calmness of mists.

The place I come from hangs sea
salty in tears from iron rails
painted in two tones of blue and rusted
through and through: painted
over and over.

Over the railway's easy shuckle,
between the lover's clasp,
wound around the wheels of cars,
drizzled through the pub door's chatter,
in the breath-drawn gape of the yard cat's yowl
and splintered in the uncertainty of the last bus wait
the North Sea flexes its muscle.

Sand and blood, colder there, knitted
in the net fixed by a fisherman for the next day's shot
and caught in his wife's stingray stare. The sea
ALWAYS
            uncomfortable like a learning child.

The Fifties, Ten Miles East of Newcastle.

Shipyards nodding craned heads
say, "Yes!"
to post-war workers
oily for money.

A teenager chews gum
trying like hell
to look dangerous
outside the *American Pastimes*

amusement arcade. A leverage
of James Dean,
denim jeans and Presley
dehisce *Coca-Cola* tops.

The Spanish City rocks
The Big Bopper;
rolls the Big Dipper
and jive.

Drainpipe legs leak
in the sharpest shoes
or puddle in crepe
- dubious as a hairdo.

Popcorn!
Plastic!
Formica!
Automatic!

Somebody tells me
The States are great.
My mouth buckles,
"Yeah."

Curiosity Kills The Cats.

There's a gathering.
A fight? No, just Them.
They're finger-dipping
expensive sherbet again.

Out in the open
the onsell of dust
like we used to swap cards
but this ain't kids' stuff.

The policeman said,
"This is not kids' stuff!"
The headmaster said,
"This isn't kids' stuff!"

Those kids want it 'cos
it ain't kids' stuff.

A21/M25/M1/M18.

Foot to the floor for five hours;
the lights blur.

Cassettes on the passenger seat a mountain
of boredom: the ignored radio plays.

The fascia display winks Chernobyl green
as another service station rainbows by.

In headlights the first holograms of glass harden,
fizzzzzzz ... pop ... zzzzzzap ...

A meteor storm of fast debris like a screen-save
and mad angled headlights searching the heavens.

Bee Cartography.

An implosion of silence ...
A leaching of light ...
Decomposition of air
into atoms of insects.

This encyclopaedic wonder
moves like Ptolemy's hand
over a white page of wall
mapping the known world.

A square Iberia tapers into India,
swelling pregnant to Africa,
slimming at ankle, makes South America.

A sill strikes away
like the peninsula of California
then frizzles fierce as fat and water
and shrinks, coy as Surtsey.

Hedges.

Hedges intrigue me.
They wear their green like personality
over a madness of twigs.

Shaped by hands
they adopt regimental straightness and can
arch, sphere; peacock in topiary.

Unobserved the renegade awaits
the chance to redefine shape;
to reinvent the line.

The sense of solitude was immense. I could not see or realise my own body, and I seemed to exist only in my perception of the waves and of the crying birds, and of the smell of seaweed.

J M Synge
(The Aran Islands)

Thirteen of Lindisfarne
for Graham Hartill

1

wood smoked dusk and rowed to the island
oars slicing loaf waves

knives of dune grass
shred the touching sky

wind heckles
naming brethren in its slit craw

C - th - bt

a green-stenched shore cloys
as light hangs by seconds

the evening beach blackened
under stools of upturned boats

woodsmokesaintsalt

the scrape of keel on sand
surf hissing
its greedy tongue
up   &   down
wet openings

2

wing-stiff on a mattress of air
a lump-brown gull issues challenge
head down and sweeping
side-to-side
its bullying cry
has a life of seconds

devoured then by gale
and by sea this island's pule
rises with the tide
inflates in the wind
breaks with the day
brittles the night
slides down slates
chases the boat
crowns the rock

hunts the half-seas over fisherman
along short-strung streets
it is Ahab
weatherlashed along the isle's whale rolled back

3

eyes and ears and jumbled language land
to work a way
worm into wood
ingesting past and present

the mead blending does well
the monks would approve
this marketing

illuminated labels authenticate
bottles
toffee
fudge

such is
THE WORD
purchased
shrink-wrapped within the twentieth century

soft computer touch

4

mollusc on a sill of whin
a castle whorls its enclosed world
making mystery its captive
so little of reality escapes
so much of the mind goes in

a stranger has memories returned
a climbed wall
mirrored water

mars
venus
mercury
tiptoe upon time

furled cloaks
spilt sea
curled air
so little soil to set a colony

hardly enough for *fearn* to grow
to cut and carpet floor
or dry
tinder-ready
for wild winter hearths to roar

relentless the sea
awash
awash
wet gaoling
and blinding fret
boats kept beached

fearn: Old English for fern. Bracken was used for a floor covering as early as Roman Times. Some believe Farne to be a corruption of *fearn*. Lindisfarne: *lin - aeceras* (Old English) = flax fields. Professor Eilert Ekwall has it as a colony of people from Lindis, the name for North Lincolnshire.

6

The sea is both monger and mean thief
selling and retrieving its store
all but capturing this small land
in wet temper

it works a sound
sturm und drang

ceaseless
slid sand
raked stones
sickle waves
successive
restless
coils of sea wreathe
beneath the gull's gelid eye

a local tells this tale

a caad neet pallatic from the yelhoose
heor n theor
tottad davy-dando heyem
with a wrang word
n dunchin var nigh aal the doors
n faalin doon
swayin like a shuggyboat
a sang ripenin is lips
nivva maikn much but a spitty gargle

anaall the time
the dark neet hid a geet big worm
slitherun gigantic ower the foreshore
till davy met it face to face

whey man in his state
ee thowtit glamerus
thowt its twinklyee
a charm

afore lang the twowor back at the yelhoose
arm in arm
clammin fara drink
emptyin it   pubnaal

whey man so it was ivvor nowt alcoholic was left
sept davy dando deed on the flowa
na broken hearted worm var nigh pickled
thet drooned its wrigglysel lovesick off bamburgh
leavin its humpyback faships twreckthemsels
fa toorist tcaal the farnes

8

the gull is a coat-hanger
suspended in the turbulence
gyroscopically still

tilted & turned
the world thrashes beneath

the island is map-flat
though grass stroked like fur to the nap of foreshore
works its obedience to the wind

determined to blow itself out
the bluster chases its ghost over land and sea
whipping a wave
curling back the crest
as a mane tossed in stampede

an eel of colour slidders
after the heading-home boat
over the drowning sea
on which floats

a jigsaw of this
a flotilla of that
a raft of ducks
beads of buoys to mark crab traps

islands of short term
awash
awash

two cries lost
the gull veers off

9

there is a temperature change
a fever rising with the sea's ebb

riding down hard
islanders
young bucks and old hands
escape between exploded water-zips

trucks are broncos
bucking up from scattered rocks
hootin-tootin-horns
out to rodeo
from beal to budle bay

10

an undone button
on a plissé sea
hangs by a thread
between tides
on which people ply
back and forth
to and fro
come and go
as if in running repair

11

much is in ruin
or heading there
only where inhabitation smoulders
do buildings show sparks of repair

the bones of a priory
moan no prayer
the wind only
takes its aeolian fancy
where once its timbre shrank
from christian clarion

time
a high
and low-water
rictus

the past
a sound
howled and whispered

12

out of season
visitors eat sandwiches
in the church of a coach

the weather unwelcome

though this island knows
the percolation of folk
the raider
the wrecked
the hunted
the hermit

lindisfarne
at once no place and home
for the xenophobic

13

thought and prayer are islands
and not

images ink the mind

christianity's cruciform casts its shadow

the wind calls
the gull echoes
the child learns
the man remembers how

Ten of Place.

i
An artist's impression
of the Moon ... I
                    have been there.

ii
Malacca - coco-de-mer bent over whetstone sands, sickled by sea -

a catfish breeze slippery through grass;
the prayer-wind *Allah* the palm branch,
                    Allah.

iii
Tolon: resort music dusted uphill. A sea breeze
settles on the glass lip of ouzo.

iv
Athens: debris of cancelled flights. Bewildered
mothers try to toilet; keep sanitary, their children
wild in a playground. Everywhere
armed soldiers, more people
exhausted over luggage adrift of care,
place themselves in the hands of the authorities.
The stench of *terrible* history.

v
Loro Park / Puerto de la Cruz: the brilliant parrot replies,
"Hello!"
My three year old daughter doesn't know
what to do, but run to her mother. No other
bird repeats this.

    The child is disappointed;
confused; begins to be unsure; needs
to return to the first cage.

"Hello?"
"Hello!"

My young daughter then trusts that word once more.
That word I understand

     and discover its gift.

vi
Uncounted grains compose one mile of Tynemouth Long Sands
- its shifting, up and down, almost invisible - the colour
undisturbed. A single cannon-shot stone
picked up; snuggled into the neck.

The arm latent with thrust, waits ...

fires the rock.

Into emptiness a boy runs.
How sudden a place is filled.

vii
Cullercoats Bay: from outside each cave is a vault of mystery.
                    Inside, each is dark and smells of shit.

viii
The Philippino boys roast a pig
stuck through mouth to arse by a spit.
One turns the carcass slowly over
a lake of embers and drinks bottled beer.

Birani is the senior brother and caretaker
for the millionaire's house high on the cliff
above Las Salinas, on the south side of the island.
Here they sear the pig; fire their fast words and smiles,

move their dark eyes over all things
as if counting: make this place familiar.
Time after time each turns his head, presses
finger and thumb hard into eyes, says, "*Humo*!"

Later the flesh is stripped and night brightens
the hunks of charred wood. Now their eyes only
show white and fingernails' lustre pearl crescents.
They eat; stare bang into the unyielding blackness.

humo = smoke
the island is Ibiza

ix
Hen & Chickens, Abergavenny, *a home to poetry*,
Flannel Street, Tuesdays, upstairs.

Thoughts mix: the sting and jellyfish ballet.

P.A. substandard - often
                                    not used.
Everyone hears what they want.
1st,   2nd,   3rd   silence.

                              (*Moku*)

                              x
                              Without,
                              no place but self.

Moku = silence
1st silence is that of ignorance
2nd silence is a pretence of ignorance
3rd silence is knowledge that the subject cannot be explained. Hence silence.

Square One.

i *Back, from Beckley, to Blaina.*

Diary 1998: Return, the warm home chilled by absence; marble-silent,
tidy as last left, 'cept the mail, grown across the hall and crimped
under the opened door, ready to be sorted like a card trick.
Defibrillation, click, click, electronic
systems booted and cold displays wink for attention.
Hello! My voiceprint back. The walls recall;
the Spanish mirror gets me
in full vision.

Yesterday's even fields hoisted to a mountain.
A window frames an oblong of bracken and like
projection a watery light dances only
a hinted me, silent onto a painted wall. Today

another page in a book of changes -
a wash / different clothes.

ii *From Darkness*

Diary: Bad night.

Seconds of water (hear them!) drip.
Delicate explosions give away locations
darkness fails to disguise and insomnia tries
to reject.

      The destroyer swims deltaic above *coiffured* artex,
a Nile into the Mediterranean of my bedroom, washing
grit to deposits which puncture first morning steps.

Diary: Phone calls, many calls, for help! Wait.

Young voices, clinical, operational,
diet on details - postcode and claim's number.

Real response is slow.

Nile turns Victoria.

Cups of capture;
      bucket;
      basin;
      bowl.

      Moveables - bed, wardrobe, desk - to dry ground.

Try
to find the source. Logical;
geographical to trace
back.

Diary: No entry.

iii *To Light.*

Mother has an open reference
from Shell Oil Co., South Africa,
dated 1945.
She is proud of it and shows
the letter. I think of
this
each time I fill with petrol. The evaporation
ripples back -
octane has me as high as Mum.
Her film-star-face in ecstatic youth
alive
each time she shows the letterhead.

T' make her face, impossible. At that time
when sepia barely coped, colour, then,
would have captured not her, but iridescence.
This diamond - no,
this woman.

Diary. Insurance green light. Builders - much mess.
Never on time. Many phone calls and careful words. Keep calm ... time.
Mothers' Day soon.

Running tearfully after her as she escaped house-tension,
thinking she would go; knowing
I couldn't let her.

A picnic on the front lawn
in summer after school.

How she made things WORK. The walks
'cross the rocks from Cullercoats,
'round Brown's Point, by the wreck, searching
every rock pool to Rockcliff.
A sea breeze billowing her checked frock
thro' the village, home.

A jumper handed over the school wall as the day chilled.

The front door pushed easily. The sound crinkled -
like the door-case's copper strip - in my memory.

My universe, a few acres of land;
a tidal margin of fun
from which Foxton Avenue was sprinting distance;
number 30 the end of the race.

Radiance!
Yellow, yellow, days, sand, swimming trunks,
kitchen, tinned pineapple, eggs ...

simple as an illusion.

iv Almost Losing The Music.

In me everything of the river. I have
splashed over the rock bed of youth, dashed
fantastically without purpose and felt
the stun
of each outcrop.

Eric Burdon opened the door:
We Got To Get Outa This Place,
to find the way home by the journey outward.

Restless liquid teens spurted - London
        and beyond, the valley
stretched into the arid emptiness of Spain.
That dry blade bleeding the river.

Remembered Bella Taylor selling winkles
from a Bank Top stall, singing
her trade. The last Cullercoats' Fishwife.

Too, St. Mary's Lighthouse
distant and close as its beam
wielded like a claymore to slice the night,
the short distance to shore and out
to scar the far horizon.

place   As employed in HUMANIST GEOGRAPHY,
        place refers to that geographical space
        occupied by a person or object.   *Modern Dictionary of
Geography*

The river can never return to source
                nor ever lose it.

I hear the music
                        again
a clattering rapid: MacSweeney, Shearer, Shearer...

Diary: New roof. *Kika Onza.*

Kika Onza = returning to the original home

Acknowledgements.

Acknowledgements are due to the editors of the following magazines and anthologies in which some of the poems first appeared: *New Welsh Review; Borderlines; 4 Words; Wisdom of the Crocodiles; Of Sawn Grain; Fire; Private People; First Times.*

also by the author

Making It	isbn	1 899449 45 0
Tilt	isbn	1 899449 30 2

About   # The Collective

e-mail   john.jones6@which.net

The Collective is a non profit making organisation formed in 1990 to promote and publish contemporary poetry. Funds are raised through a series of poetry events held in and around South Wales, mainly the Abergavenny area. The backing and generosity of fellow writers is a cornerstone of The Collective's success. Vital funding comes from public bodies including the Arts Council of Wales and donations are often received in support of the movement from members of the public. If you would like to find out more about The Collective and its work then contact:

The Co-ordinator
The Collective
Penlanlas Farm
Llantilio Pertholey
Y-Fenni
Gwent
NP7 7HN

fish